THIS PLANNER BELONGS TO:

_____

_____

COPYRIGHT

TABLE OF CONTENTS

INTRODUCTION

Welcome to your Peace of Mind and Heart Planners.

This book is designed to make life-planning as simple, user friendly, and stress-free as possible.

Your Planner is a comprehensive, customizable, all-in-one workbook to record your vital information, personal wishes, and final messages to loved ones.

It is a valuable gift for those left behind so that they can ensure your instructions are fulfilled accordingly, and to help avoid duress or confusion by planning in advance.

We have provided plenty of space to customize each section as per your needs, and include additional overflow space at the end of the book if required. It is helpful to begin with the initial personal identification section first, and then proceed to one chapter at a time, collecting all the documentation and information in advance for efficiency sake.

Remember to update this planner as changes to your circumstances arise, such as new employment, investments, insurance, or adjustments to your personal wishes.

Please remember, this planner is not considered a legal document and should not be considered a formal will.

*Always store this workbook somewhere safe, to prevent sensitive, private information from getting into the wrong hands.

PERSONAL INFORMATION

Legal Name

_____

_____

_____

Address

_____

_____

_____

Mailbox or P.O. Box Number

_____

_____

Mailbox Location

_____

_____

Key Location

_____

_____

_____

Primary Phone Numbers

_____

_____

_____

_____

Family Members

Spouse's Name / Maiden Name

_____

_____

Children's Names

_____

_____

_____

_____

_____

_____

_____

_____

Grandchildren's Names

_____

_____

_____

_____

_____

_____

_____

_____

My Dependents Names Include

_____

_____

_____

_____

_____

_____

_____

_____

Pet Names

_____

_____

_____

_____

Notes

_____

_____

_____

_____

_____

Siblings Names

_____

_____

_____

_____

_____

_____

Mother's Name / Maiden Name

_____

_____

Father's Name

_____

_____

Ex-Spouse's Name/s

_____

_____

_____

Notes

_____

_____

_____

_____

AT THE TIME OF PASSING

Please Contact the Following People Immediately Upon My Passing or Incapacity

Spouse / Partner

Name

Contact Information

Notes

Healthcare Power of Attorney Agent

Name

Contact Information

Notes

Executor of Will

Name

Contact Information

Notes

Please Contact the Following People

Mentor

Place of Worship _____

Contact Information _____

Notes _____

_____

_____

_____

Mentor 2

Church Name _____

Contact Information _____

Notes _____

_____

_____

Admin/Associate #1

Name _____

Contact Information _____

Notes _____

_____

_____

Admin/Associate #2

Name _____

Contact Information _____

Notes _____

_____

_____

Please Contact the Following Family, Friends, and Associates

Name

Contact Information

Relationship

Name

Contact Information

Relationship

Name

Contact Information

Relationship

Name

Contact Information

Relationship

Name

Contact Information

Relationship

Name

Contact Information

Relationship

Name

Contact Information

Relationship

Notes

Please Contact the Following Family, Friends, and Associates

Name

Contact Information

Relationship

Name

Contact Information

Relationship

Name

Contact Information

Relationship

Name

Contact Information

Relationship

Name

Contact Information

Relationship

Name

Contact Information

Relationship

Name

Contact Information

Relationship

Notes

Please Contact the Following Family, Friends, and Associates

Name

Contact Information

Relationship

Name

Contact Information

Relationship

Name

Contact Information

Relationship

Name

Contact Information

Relationship

Name

Contact Information

Relationship

Name

Contact Information

Relationship

Name

Contact Information

Relationship

Notes

Please Contact the Following Family, Friends, and Associates

Name

Contact Information

Relationship

Name

Contact Information

Relationship

Name

Contact Information

Relationship

Name

Contact Information

Relationship

Name

Contact Information

Relationship

Name

Contact Information

Relationship

Name

Contact Information

Relationship

Notes

Additional Key Contact Information

Accountant and Book Keeper

Name #1 _____

Contact Information _____

Name #2 _____

Contact Information _____

Notes _____

_____

Lawyer #1

Name _____

Contact Information _____

Notes _____

_____

Lawyer #2

Name _____

Contact Information _____

Notes _____

_____

Estate Planner

Name _____

Contact Information _____

Notes _____

_____

Financial Planner

Company and Agent Name _____

Contact Information _____

Financial Planner

Company and Agent Name _____

Contact Information _____

Stock Broker

Company and Agent Name _____

Contact Information _____

Business Employer / Associate

Company and Agent Name _____

Contact Information _____

Business Employer / Associate

Company and Agent Name _____

Contact Information _____

Business Employer / Associate

Company and Agent Name _____

Contact Information _____

Notes _____

Health Care Provider – Medical

Company and Agent Name

Contact Information

Health Care Provider – Dental

Company and Agent Name

Contact Information

Health Care Provider – Vision

Company and Agent Name

Contact Information

Health Care Provider – Other

Company and Agent Name

Contact Information

Veterinarian

Company and Agent Name

Contact Information

Veterinarian

Company and Agent Name

Contact Information

Notes

FUNERAL ARRANGEMENTS

Funeral Arrangements Contact Person

Location

Contact Information

Place of Worship

Primary Contact

Contact Information

Funeral Home

Address

Contact Information

Cemetery or Crematorium

Plot / Address

Contact Information

Funeral Insurance Policy

Company Name

Contact Information

Notes

Burial

Headstone Details

Cremation

Ashes to be shared with / spread at

Obituary

Please Include the Following

Funeral Arrangements - Celebration of Life Services

Please Read the Following Farewell to My Loved Ones During Service (Values, Lessons, Encouragement, Etc.)

Funeral Arrangements – Notes

PLACE OF WORSHIP

Place of Worship - Instructions

Place of Worship - Instructions

Charities

Tithing

Legacy & Other Related Topics

Legacy & Other Related Topics

Notes

ASSETS OVERVIEW – WHAT MY LOVED ONES CAN EXPECT

Personal Residence Address

Note: Please see will for detailed instructions and division of assets

_____

_____

_____

_____

PO Box Location and Address

_____

_____

_____

Partner / Co-Owner Names

_____

_____

_____

Contact Information

_____

_____

_____

Legal Will Location and Instructions for Division of Assets

_____

_____

_____

_____

_____

_____

Keys Location and Miscellaneous Instructions

Alarm and Security Information

Utilities Warranties and Documentation Location

Upkeep Information and Document Location (Gardener, Etc.)

Notes

Real Estate Investment - Second Property Address

Type of Property (Residential / Commercial)

PO Box Location and Address

Partner / Co-Owner Names

Contact Information

Legal Documentation Location and Instructions

Keys Location and Miscellaneous Instructions

Alarm and Security Information

Utilities Warranties and Documentation Location

Upkeep Information and Document Location (Gardener, Etc.)

Notes

Vehicle List: Car, Motorcycle, Recreation Vehicle, Snowmobile, Etc.

Vehicle

Year/Make/Model

VIN – ID

Ownership Documentation Location

Lease / Load Information

Keys Location

Notes

Vehicle

Year/Make/Model

VIN – ID

Ownership Documentation Location

Lease / Load Information

Keys Location

Notes

Vehicle List:

Vehicle _____

Year/Make/Model _____

_____

VIN – ID _____

Ownership Documentation Location _____

Lease / Load Information _____

Keys Location _____

Notes _____

_____

_____

_____

_____

Vehicle _____

Year/Make/Model _____

_____

VIN – ID _____

Ownership Documentation Location _____

Lease / Load Information _____

Keys Location _____

Notes _____

_____

_____

_____

_____

Vehicle List:

Vehicle

Year/Make/Model

VIN – ID

Ownership Documentation Location

Lease / Load Information

Keys Location

Notes

Vehicle

Year/Make/Model

VIN – ID

Ownership Documentation Location

Lease / Load Information

Keys Location

Notes

Investments: Stocks, Mutual Funds, and Other

Type

Location

Account Number

Contact Person

Documentation Location

Notes

Type

Location

Account Number

Contact Person

Documentation Location

Notes

Type

Location

Account Number

Contact Person

Documentation Location

Notes

Investments:

Type

Location

Account Number

Contact Person

Documentation Location

Notes

Type

Location

Account Number

Contact Person

Documentation Location

Notes

Type

Location

Account Number

Contact Person

Documentation Location

Notes

Investments:

Type

Location

Account Number

Contact Person

Documentation Location

Notes

Type

Location

Account Number

Contact Person

Documentation Location

Notes

Type

Location

Account Number

Contact Person

Documentation Location

Notes

Insurance Benefits:

Policy Type _____

Location _____

Account Number _____

Contact Person _____

Documentation Location _____

Notes _____

_____

_____

Policy Type _____

Location _____

Account Number _____

Contact Person _____

Documentation Location _____

Notes _____

_____

_____

Policy Type _____

Location _____

Account Number _____

Contact Person _____

Documentation Location _____

Notes _____

_____

Employer Benefits #1

Name

Account Number

Contact Person

Documentation Location

Notes

Employer Benefits #2

Name

Account Number

Contact Person

Documentation Location

Notes

Employer Benefits #3

Name

Account Number

Contact Person

Documentation Location

Notes

Retirement Benefits

Name

Account Number

Contact Person

Documentation Location

Notes

Retirement Benefits #2

Name

Account Number

Contact Person

Documentation Location

Notes

Social Security

Name

Account Number

Contact Person

Documentation Location

Notes

Other: Veteran's Benefits, Etc.

Name

Account Number

Contact Person

Documentation Location

Notes

Other:

Name

Account Number

Contact Person

Documentation Location

Notes

Other:

Name

Account Number

Contact Person

Documentation Location

Notes

Money Owed to Me

Name

Account Number

Contact Person

Documentation Location

Notes

Name

Account Number

Contact Person

Documentation Location

Notes

Name

Account Number

Contact Person

Documentation Location

Notes

Personal Items, Jewelry, and Heirlooms

Item

Location

Notes

Item

Location

Notes

Item

Location

Notes

Item

Location

Notes

Personal Items, Jewelry, and Heirlooms

Item

Location

Notes

Item

Location

Notes

Item

Location

Notes

Item

Location

Notes

Personal Items, Jewelry, and Heirlooms

Item

Location

Notes

Item

Location

Notes

Item

Location

Notes

Item

Location

Notes

Personal Items, Jewelry, and Heirlooms

Item

Location

Notes

Item

Location

Notes

Item

Location

Notes

Item

Location

Notes

Storage Company #1

Name

Address

Key Location or Combination Number

Storage Company #2

Name

Address

Key Location or Combination Number

Notes and Instructions

BUSINESS INFORMATION

Business Details

Business Name

Business Type

Address

Landlord Name

Contact Information

Lease Documentation Location

Partner / Co-Owner Name

Contact Information

Partner / Co-Owner Name

Contact Information

Partner / Co-Owner Name

Contact Information

Partner / Co-Owner Name

Contact Information

Keys Location

Notes

Associates, Employees, and Contractors

Name

Contact Information

Name

Contact Information

Name

Contact Information

Name

Contact Information

Name

Contact Information

Name

Contact Information

Name

Contact Information

Name

Contact Information

Notes

Business Information

Name

Contact Information

Name

Contact Information

Name

Contact Information

Name

Contact Information

Name

Contact Information

Name

Contact Information

Name

Contact Information

Name

Contact Information

Notes

Bank Name

Address

Contact Information

Business Bank Account Number

Business Bank Account Number

Credit Card Number

Username / PIN

Credit Card Number

Username / PIN

Documentation Location

Notes

Bank Name

Address

Contact Information

Business Bank Account Number

Business Bank Account Number

Credit Card Number

Username / PIN

Credit Card Number

Username / PIN

Documentation Location

Notes

Business Information

Accountant Name

Contact Information

Lawyer

Contact Information

Insurance Agency / Agent

Contact Information

Notes on Income, Royalties, Key Accounts Etc.

Online Business Information

Business Website Name

Hosting Provider

Username and Password

Website Developer Name

Contact Information

Documentation Location

Online Income Stream #1

Online Income Stream #2

Partner / Co-Owner Name

Contact Information

Partner / Co-Owner Name

Contact Information

Partner / Co-Owner Name

Contact Information

Business Email Address Name

Username and Password

Business Email Address Name

Username and Password

Business Email Address Name

Username and Password

Notes

Notes: Instructions for Domain Name Renewal, Hosting, Expenses, Etc.

Social Media

Name

Username and Password

Name

Username and Password

Name

Username and Password

Name

Username and Password

Name

Username and Password

Name

Username and Password

Name

Username and Password

Name

Username and Password

Name

Username and Password

Accounts

Name

Username and Password

Name

Username and Password

Name

Username and Password

Name

Username and Password

Name

Username and Password

Name

Username and Password

Name

Username and Password

Name

Username and Password

Name

Username and Password

Name

Username and Password

Money I Owe to Others

Person / Company Name

Contact Information

Documentation Location

Notes

Person / Company Name

Contact Information

Documentation Location

Notes

Person / Company Name

Contact Information

Documentation Location

Notes

Person / Company Name

Contact Information

Documentation Location

Notes

Additional Notes

Additional Notes and Instructions

BANKING INFORMATION

Note: Please secure this document due to its sensitive information, (ideally in a safe), or place specific sensitive information somewhere separate with instructions to access as desired.

Bank Name

Account Type and Number

Account Type and Number

Bank Online Web Address

Username and Password

Debit Card Number

Credit Card Number

CV and Password

Online Username and Password

Rewards

Notes

Bank Name

Account Type and Number

Account Type and Number

Bank Online Web Address

Username and Password

Debit Card Number

Credit Card Number

CV and Password

Online Username and Password

Rewards

Notes

Bank Name

Account Type and Number

Account Type and Number

Bank Online Web Address

Username and Password

Debit Card Number

Credit Card Number

CV and Password

Online Username and Password

Rewards

Notes

Safe Deposit Box

Bank Location

Box Number

Key Location

Contents

Safe Deposit Box

Bank Location

Box Number

Key Location

Contents

Other Credit: Credit Cards, Line of Credit, Department Stores, Etc.

Name

Account Number

Online Website

Username and Password

Name

Account Number

Online Website

Username and Password

Name

Account Number

Online Website

Username and Password

Name

Account Number

Online Website

Username and Password

Name

Account Number

Online Website

Username and Password

Notes

Other Credit: Credit Cards, Line of Credit, Department Stores, Etc.

Name

Account Number

Online Website

Username and Password

Name

Account Number

Online Website

Username and Password

Name

Account Number

Online Website

Username and Password

Name

Account Number

Online Website

Username and Password

Name

Account Number

Online Website

Username and Password

Notes

Other Credit: Credit Cards, Line of Credit, Department Stores, Etc.

Name

Account Number

Online Website

Username and Password

Name

Account Number

Online Website

Username and Password

Name

Account Number

Online Website

Username and Password

Name

Account Number

Online Website

Username and Password

Name

Account Number

Online Website

Username and Password

Notes

Mortgage, Line of Credit, Loans

Mortgage Details

Bank / Lender

Contact Information

Account Number

Documentation Location

Second Mortgage Details

Bank / Lender

Contact Information

Account Number

Documentation Location

Third Mortgage Details

Bank / Lender

Contact Information

Account Number

Documentation Location

Other

Bank / Lender

Contact Information

Account Number

Documentation Location

Notes

Line of Credit

Bank / Lender

Contact Information

Account Number

Documentation Location

Line of Credit

Bank / Lender

Contact Information

Account Number

Documentation Location

Other

Bank / Lender

Contact Information

Account Number

Documentation Location

Other

Bank / Lender

Contact Information

Account Number

Documentation Location

Notes

Loans: Cars, Student Loan, Etc.

Bank / Lender

Contact Information

Account Number

Documentation Location

Bank / Lender

Contact Information

Account Number

Documentation Location

Bank / Lender

Contact Information

Account Number

Documentation Location

Bank / Lender

Contact Information

Account Number

Documentation Location

Bank / Lender

Contact Information

Account Number

Documentation Location

Notes

IMPORTANT DOCUMENTATION LOCATION

Will

_____

_____

Notes _____

_____

Health Care Power of Attorney Papers

_____

Notes _____

_____

Passport

_____

Notes _____

_____

Birth Certificate

_____

_____

Notes _____

_____

_____

_____

Social Security Card

Notes

Drivers Licence

Notes

Marriage Certificate

Notes

Tax Documents

Notes

Divorce Papers

Notes

Life Insurance

Notes

Health Insurance - Medical

Notes

Health Insurance Location – Dental

Notes

Health Insurance Location - Vision

Notes

Health Insurance Location – Other

Notes

Funeral Insurance

Notes

Vehicle Insurance #1

Notes

Vehicle Insurance #2

Notes

Vehicle Insurance #3

Notes

Home Owner Insurance

Notes

Rental Home Insurance

Notes

Children's Insurance #1

Notes

Children's Insurance #2

Notes

Children's Insurance #3

Notes

Other Family / Dependents Insurance

Notes

Pet Insurance #1

Notes

Pet Insurance #2

Notes

Storage Insurance #1

Notes

Storage Insurance #2

Notes

Additional Notes

Important Documents Location

Other

_____

_____

Notes

Other

_____

_____

Notes

Other

_____

_____

Notes

Other

_____

_____

Notes

Other

_____

_____

Notes

Other

_____

_____

Notes

_____

Important Documents Location - Notes

INSURANCE PROVIDER INFORMATION

Health Insurance – Primary Health

Company Name

Agents Name

Contact Information

HSA (Health Savings Account) Information

Health Insurance - Dental

Company Name

Agents Name

Contact Information

Notes

Health Insurance – Vision

Company Name

Agents Name

Contact Information

Notes

Health Insurance – Medical

Company Name

Agents Name

Contact Information

Notes

Additional Notes

Life Insurance #1

Company Name

Agents Name

Contact Information

Notes

Life Insurance #2

Company Name

Agents Name

Contact Information

Notes

Vehicle Insurance #1

Company Name

Agents Name

Contact Information

Notes

Vehicle Insurance #2

Company Name

Agents Name

Contact Information

Notes

Vehicle Insurance #3

Company Name

Agents Name

Notes

Home Owner Insurance

Company Name

Agents Name

Contact Information

Notes

Rental Home Insurance

Company Name

Agents Name

Contact Information

Notes

Children's Insurance #1

Company Name

Agents Name

Contact Information

Notes

Children's Insurance #2

Company Name

Agents Name

Contact Information

Notes

Children's Insurance #3

Company Name

Agents Name

Contact Information

Notes

Other Dependents Insurance

Company Name

Agents Name

Contact Information

Notes

Pet Insurance #1

Company Name

Vets Name

Contact Information

Notes

Pet Insurance #2

Company Name

Vets Name

Contact Information

Notes

Storage Insurance #1

Company Name

Agents Name

Contact Information

Notes

Storage Insurance #2

Company Name

Agents Name

Contact Information

Notes

Funeral Insurance

Company Name

Agents Name

Contact Information

Notes

Other Insurance

Company Name

Agents Name

Contact Information

Notes

Other Insurance

Company Name

Agents Name

Contact Information

Notes

Other Insurance

Company Name

Agents Name

Contact Information

Notes

Other Insurance

Company Name

Agents Name

Contact Information

Notes

MEDICAL INFORMATION

Health Care Power of Attorney

Name

Contact Information

Notes

Do Not Resuscitate Instructions Document Location

Notes

Organ Donor Instructions Document Location

Notes

Blood Type

Primary Care Physician

Name

Contact Information

Address

Notes

Medical Conditions

Medications

Allergies, Food Sensitivity, and Reactions

If Incapacitated Please Follow Below Requests (Further Details in DNR Document)

Preferred Hospital

Name

Contact Information

Address

Notes

Pharmacy

Name

Contact Information

Address

Notes

Caregiver Company / Person #1

Name

Contact Information

Address

Notes

Caregiver Company / Person #2

Name

Contact Information

Address

Notes

Medical Information - Notes

DEPENDENTS & INSTRUCTIONS OF CARE

My Dependents

Name

Relationship

Contact Information

Personal Documentation Location

Health Conditions Documentation Location

Guardianship Instructions Documentation Location

Guardian Name

Contact Information

Primary Care Physician

Contact Information

Notes

My Dependents

Name

Relationship

Contact Information

Personal Documentation Location

Health Conditions Documentation Location

Guardianship Instructions Documentation Location

Guardian Name

Contact Information

Primary Care Physician

Contact Information

Notes

My Dependents

Name

Relationship

Contact Information

Personal Documentation Location

Health Conditions Documentation Location

Guardianship Instructions Documentation Location

Guardian Name

Contact Information

Primary Care Physician

Contact Information

Notes

My Dependents

Name

Relationship

Contact Information

Personal Documentation Location

Health Conditions Documentation Location

Guardianship Instructions Documentation Location

Guardian Name

Contact Information

Primary Care Physician

Contact Information

Notes

My Dependents

Name

Relationship

Contact Information

Personal Documentation Location

Health Conditions Documentation Location

Guardianship Instructions Documentation Location

Guardian Name

Contact Information

Primary Care Physician

Contact Information

Notes

My Dependents

Name

Relationship

Contact Information

Personal Documentation Location

Health Conditions Documentation Location

Guardianship Instructions Documentation Location

Guardian Name

Contact Information

Primary Care Physician

Contact Information

Notes

My Dependents – Pets

Name / Type of Pet

Name of Veterinarian

Contact Information

Address

License, Insurance, and Documentation Location

Health Conditions

Medications

Guardianship Instructions Documentation Location

Guardian Name

Contact Information

General Instructions of Care – Food, Habits, Exercise, Sleep, and Other Needs

My Dependents – Pets

Name / Type of Pet

Name of Veterinarian

Contact Information

Address

License, Insurance, and Documentation Location

Health Conditions

Medications

Guardianship Instructions Documentation Location

Guardian Name

Contact Information

General Instructions of Care – Food, Habits, Exercise, Sleep, and Other Needs

My Dependents – Pets

Name / Type of Pet

Name of Veterinarian

Contact Information

Address

License, Insurance, and Documentation Location

Health Conditions

Medications

Guardianship Instructions Documentation Location

Guardian Name

Contact Information

General Instructions of Care – Food, Habits, Exercise, Sleep, and Other Needs

My Dependents – Notes

LOOSE ENDS TO TIE UP

Follow Up: Cancel, Close, Pay, Change of Name, Etc.

Example: Hydro, Electric, Phone, Cable, Internet, Storage, Credit Cards, Autopay, Banking...

Company

Contact Information

Account Number

Username and Password

Notes

Company

Contact Information

Account Number

Username and Password

Notes

Company

Contact Information

Account Number

Username and Password

Notes

Company

Contact Information

Account Number

Username and Password

Notes

Company

Contact Information

Account Number

Username and Password

Notes

Company

Contact Information

Account Number

Username and Password

Notes

Company

Contact Information

Account Number

Username and Password

Notes

Company

Contact Information

Account Number

Username and Password

Notes

Company

Contact Information

Account Number

Username and Password

Notes

Company

Contact Information

Account Number

Username and Password

Notes

Company

Contact Information

Account Number

Username and Password

Notes

Company

Contact Information

Account Number

Username and Password

Notes

Loose Ends to Tie Up Online:

Email, Website, Hosting, Social Media, Banking, Amazon eBay, Memberships

Company

Contact Information

Account Number

Username and Password

Notes

Company

Contact Information

Account Number

Username and Password

Notes

Company

Contact Information

Account Number

Username and Password

Notes

Company

Contact Information

Account Number

Username and Password

Notes

Loose Ends to Tie Up Online:

Company _____

Contact Information _____

Account Number _____

Username and Password _____

Notes _____

_____

Company _____

Contact Information _____

Account Number _____

Username and Password _____

Notes _____

_____

Company _____

Contact Information _____

Account Number _____

Username and Password _____

Notes _____

_____

Company _____

Contact Information _____

Account Number _____

Username and Password _____

Notes _____

_____

Loose Ends to Tie Up Online:

Company _____

Contact Information _____

Account Number _____

Username and Password _____

Notes _____

_____

Company _____

Contact Information _____

Account Number _____

Username and Password _____

Notes _____

_____

Company _____

Contact Information _____

Account Number _____

Username and Password _____

Notes _____

_____

Company _____

Contact Information _____

Account Number _____

Username and Password _____

Notes _____

_____

MY FINAL WISHES AND INSTRUCTIONS

Final Wishes and Instructions

Final Wishes and Instructions

Final Wishes and Instructions

Final Wishes and Instructions

A MESSAGE TO MY LOVED ONES

Dear_____

I Am Always With You

Dear

I Am Always With You

Dear

I Am Always With You

Dear

I Am Always With You

Dear

I Am Always With You

Dear

I Am Always With You

Notes

Notes

Notes

Notes

Notes

Notes

SIGNATURE & DATE

LAST WORDS

_____

_____

_____

_____

_____

_____

_____

_____

_____

_____

Signature

_____

Name and Date

_____